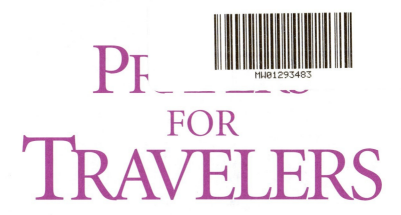

PRAYERS
FOR
TRAVELERS

ECUMENICAL AND INTERRELIGIOUS SERVICES

Endorsed by the Apostleship of the Sea
of the United States of America
(AOSUSA) for ecumenical
and interreligious use

LITURGY
TRAINING
PUBLICATIONS

PRAYERS FOR TRAVELERS: ECUMENICAL AND INTERRELIGIOUS SERVICES © 2005 Archdiocese of Chicago: Liturgy Training Publications, 1800 North Hermitage Avenue, Chicago IL 60622-1101; 1-800-933-1800, fax 1-800-933-7094, e-mail orders@ltp.org. All rights reserved. See our website at www.ltp.org.

Prayers for Travelers: Ecumenical and Interreligious Services is not intended for use by or for Roman Catholics. This book was compiled and edited by Danielle A. Knott in conjuction with the Apostleship of the Sea of the United States of America (AOUSA). Music was engraved by James T. Gerber. Carol Mycio was the production editor. The design is by M. Urgo, and the type-setting was done by Jim Mellody-Pizzato in Minion. Cover photo © 2005 Mark Hroncich.

Printed in the United States of America.

Library of Congress Control Number: 2005930750

ISBN 1-56854-596-7
PTRAV

TABLE OF CONTENTS

Introduction   v

Ecumenical Prayer Service, *Option A*   1

Ecumenical Prayer Service, *Option B*   9

Scripture Selections for Ecumenical
    Prayer Services   21

Interreligious Service   31

Renewal of Christian Marriage Vows, *Option A*   39

Renewal of Christian Marriage Vows, *Option B*   45

Scripture Selections for the Renewal
    of Christian Marriage Vows   49

Music   58

INTRODUCTION

"[An] organization concerned with the specific pastoral care of the people of the sea and seeks to support the work of believers called to give witness to their Christian life in this sphere."

—*On the Apostleship of the Sea,* Pope John Paul II

ABOUT THE APOSTLESHIP OF THE SEA

In 1920, Catholic port ministry was conceived and developed in Glasgow, Scotland, by Most Rev. Donald Macintosh, Arthur Gannon, Brother Daniel Shields, SJ, and Peter Anson, who were concerned about the lack of witness the Church was showing aboard ship. Two years later they approached Pope Pius XI, who bestowed his blessings on the ministry and encouraged the Apostleship of the Sea to extend its mission to the oceans and shores of all the hemispheres.

The mission of the Apostleship of the Sea (AOS) remains today as clear as a sailing ship's mast silhouetted against the rising sun: to reach out to seafarers, fishers, their families, and all who work at or travel on the waters and connect them to the sacramental life of the Church, especially the Eucharist. Around the world, the AOS assists seafarers to meet their basic needs: a safe work environment, a just contract, a safe haven while in port, spiritual renewal, communication with loved ones back home, a few hours of recreation, and a genuine welcome.

—The Apostleship of the Sea of the United States of America

HOW TO USE THIS BOOK

Prayers for Travelers is an easy-to-use book containing Christian and interreligious prayer services for vacationers or travelers. It has been designed to assist the preparation and prayer for both those attending and leading these services. It may be used on cruise liners, in airports, hotels, resorts, or other vacation spots as well as by those who work at sea.

To meet the needs of various denominations and faith traditions, this resource includes two ecumenical Christian services, one interreligious service, and two services for the renewal of Christian marriage vows. These services include a variety of prayers, scripture selections, meditations, and favorite hymns. The hymns may be sung a capella or accompanied by guitar, piano, or keyboard.

This resource may be used by chaplains or other designated service leaders. Even the assembly can use this book! All parts are marked for easy participation.

*May our loving God protect us on our journey
and guide us safely home.*

ECUMENICAL PRAYER SERVICE
OPTION A

Call to Worship

Opening Hymn

Music selections are found on pages 58–74.

Prayer leader:

In the name of the Father, and of the Son, and of the Holy Spirit.

All make the sign of the cross.

All: Amen.

Prayer leader:

The grace of our Lord Jesus Christ and the love of God, and the fellowship of the Holy Spirit be with you all.

All: And also with you.

Confession and Pardoning of Sin

Prayer leader:

Coming together as God's family,
with confidence let us ask the Father's forgiveness,
for he is full of gentleness and compassion.

Prayer leader:

You were sent to heal the contrite: Lord, have mercy.

All: Lord, have mercy.

You came to call sinners: Christ, have mercy.

All: Christ, have mercy.

Prayer leader:
You plead for us at the right hand of the Father:
Lord, have mercy.

All: Lord, have mercy.

Prayer leader:
May almighty God have mercy on us,
forgive us our sins,
and bring us to everlasting life.

All: Amen.

Opening Prayer

Prayer leader:
Let us pray:

Allow a moment of silent prayer.

God our Savior,
in Christ, your eternal Word,
you have revealed the full depths of your love for us.
Guide this holy assembly of your people
by the light of your Holy Spirit,
so that no word of mere human wisdom
may ever cause us to turn away from your Holy One,
the Lord, who alone has the words of eternal life,

and who lives and reigns with you
in the unity of the Holy Spirit,
God, for ever and ever.

All: Amen.

READINGS FROM THE WORD OF GOD

Scripture selections are found on pages 21–30.

Sermon/Reflection

The minister gives a sermon or reflection explaining the biblical passages proclaimed during today's service.

Hymn of the Day

Music selections are found on pages 58–74.

The Apostles' Creed

The assembly may stand for the Apostles' Creed.

Prayer leader:
Together as one family of God, we pray:

All:
I believe in God, the Father almighty,
creator of heaven and earth.

I believe in Jesus Christ, his only Son, our Lord.
He was conceived by the power of the Holy Spirit
    and born of the Virgin Mary.
he suffered under Pontius Pilate,
    was crucified, died, and was buried.
He descended to the dead.
On the third day he rose again.

He ascended into heaven,
    and is seated at the right hand of the Father.
He will come again to judge the living and the dead.

I believe in the Holy Spirit,
the holy catholic Church,
the communion of saints,
the forgiveness of sins,
the resurrection of the body,
and the life everlasting. Amen.

Prayer of the Faithful

Prayer leader:
Walking by faith, not by sight,
Let us pray with confidence to God whose kingdom
    grows among us.

A reader may be chosen to offer these or similar prayers.

Reader:
For the Church in all her communities, great and small:
May her harvest increase and her branches be large
enough to shelter all.

We pray to the Lord:

All: Lord, hear our prayer.

Reader:
For prosperous nations who have resources in
abundance: May they mirror the generosity of God
by offering a portion of their wealth and a ready
welcome to the needy.

We pray to the Lord:

All: Lord, hear our prayer.

Reader:
For those who sow the seed and nurture the fruits of the earth: May God provide a bountiful harvest for all to share.

We pray to the Lord:

All: Lord, hear our prayer.

Reader:
For those who travel: May they see God's handiwork in the splendor of wind and sea, and be renewed in spirit by their time of recreation.

We pray to the Lord:

All: Lord, hear our prayer.

Reader:
For the travelers among us: May they experience the enriching gift of hospitality.

We pray to the Lord:

All: Lord, hear our prayer.

Reader:
For those whom sickness keeps at home or for whom travel has been taken away: May God grant health and safety to all who are absent from us.

We pray to the Lord:

All: Lord, hear our prayer.

For all of us called to be part of the kingdom: May we persevere in prayer and work, trusting the God who brings great things from small beginnings.

We pray to the Lord:

All: Lord, hear our prayer.

Reader:

For those who are now at home with the Lord:
May they find mercy before the judgment seat of Christ and receive the reward of their goodness.

We pray to the Lord:

All: Lord, hear our prayer.

Prayer leader:

Loving and kind God, hear the prayers of your Church. May our voices be one with yours as we pray in the words our Savior gave us.

The Lord's Prayer

All:

Our Father, who art in heaven,
hallowed be thy name;
thy kingdom come;
thy will be done on earth as it is in heaven.
Give us this day our daily bread;
and forgive us our trespasses
as we forgive those who trespass against us;
and lead us not into temptation,
but deliver us from evil.

For the kingdom, the power and the glory are yours,
    now and for ever.

All: Amen.

Sign of Peace

Prayer leader:
As one body in Christ, let us offer to one another a sign
of peace.

The assembly offers a sign of peace to those standing nearby.

Prayer of Blessing

Prayer leader:
Let us pray:

Allow a moment of silent prayer.

All-powerful and ever-living God,
when Abraham left his own land
and departed from his own people,
you kept him safe all through his journey.
Protect us, who also are your servants:
walk by our side to help us;
be our companion and our strength on the road
and our refuge in every adversity.
Lead us, O Lord,
so that we will reach our destination in safety
and happily return to our homes.

We ask this through Christ our Lord.

All: Amen.

DISMISSAL

Prayer leader:

Let us go forth in the peace of Christ.

All: Thanks be to God!

Closing Hymn

Music selections are found on pages 58–74.

ECUMENICAL PRAYER SERVICE
OPTION B

CALL TO WORSHIP

All stand for the Call to Worship.

Prayer leader:

O God, come to my assistance.

All make the sign of the cross.

All: Lord, make haste to help me.

Prayer leader:

Glory to the Father, and to the Son,
and to the Holy Spirit:

All:

As it was in the beginning, is now, and will be for ever.
Amen.

Hymn

Music selections are found on pages 58–74.

PSALMODY

The assembly is divided into two sections: Side 1 and Side 2. Each section recites two of the following psalms in unison. All are seated for the psalmody unless otherwise noted.

Psalm 63

Side 1:

O God, you are my God, I seek you,
   my soul thirsts for you;

my flesh faints for you,
as in a dry and weary land where there is no water.

Side 2:
So I have looked upon you in the sanctuary,
beholding your power and glory.
Because your steadfast love is better than life,
my lips will praise you.
So I will bless you as long as I live;
I will lift up my hands and call on your name.

Side 1:
My soul is satisfied as with a rich feast,
and my mouth praises you with joyful lips
when I think of you on my bed,
and meditate on you in the watches of the night;
for you have been my help,
and in the shadow of your wings I sing for joy.
My soul clings to you;
your right hand upholds me.

Side 2:
But those who seek to destroy my life
shall go down into the depths of the earth;
they shall be given over to the power of the sword,
they shall be prey for jackals.

All:
But the king shall rejoice in God;
all who swear by him shall exult,
for the mouths of liars will be stopped.

All pause for a moment of silence. The minister motions for the assembly to stand and all proclaim together:

All:

Glory to the Father, and to the Son, and to the
    Holy Spirit,
As it was in the beginning, is now and will be for ever.
    Amen.

The assembly may be seated.

Psalm 100

Side 1:

Make a joyful noise to the LORD, all the earth.
    Worship the LORD with gladness;
    come into his presence with singing.

Side 2:

Know that the LORD is God.
    It is he that made us, and we are his;
    we are his people, and the sheep of his pasture.

Side 1:

Enter his gates with thanksgiving,
    and his courts with praise.
    Give thanks to him, bless his name.

Side 2:

For the LORD is good;
    his steadfast love endures forever,
    and his faithfulness to all generations.

All pause for a moment of silence. The minister motions for the assembly to stand and all proclaim together:

All:

Glory to the Father, and to the Son, and to the
  Holy Spirit,
As it was in the beginning, is now
  and will be for ever. Amen.
  The assembly may be seated.

Psalm 118

Side 1:

O give thanks to the LORD, for he is good;
 his steadfast love endures forever!

Let Israel say,
 "His steadfast love endures forever."
Let the house of Aaron say,
 "His steadfast love endures forever."
Let those who fear the LORD say,
 "His steadfast love endures forever."

Side 2:

Out of my distress I called on the LORD;
 the LORD answered me and set me in a broad place.
With the LORD on my side I do not fear.
 What can mortals do to me?

Side 1:

The LORD is on my side to help me;
 I shall look in triumph on those who hate me.
It is better to take refuge in the LORD
 than to put confidence in mortals.
It is better to take refuge in the LORD
 than to put confidence in princes.

All nations surrounded me;
  in the name of the LORD I cut them off!
They surrounded me,
surrounded me on every side;
  in the name of the LORD I cut them off!

They surrounded me like bees;
  they blazed like a fire of thorns;
  in the name of the LORD I cut them off!
I was pushed hard, so that I was falling,
  but the LORD helped me.

The LORD is my strength and my might;
  he has become my salvation.

There are glad songs of victory in the tents of
    the righteous:
  "The right hand of the LORD does valiantly;
  The right hand of the LORD is exalted;
  the right hand of the LORD does valiantly."
I shall not die, but I shall live,
  and recount the deeds of the LORD.

The LORD has punished me severely,
  but he did not give me over to death.

Open to me the gates of righteousness,
  that I may enter through them
  and give thanks to the LORD.

This is the gate of the LORD;
  the righteous shall enter through it.

Side 2:
I thank you that you have answered me
  and have become my salvation.
The stone that the builders rejected
  has become the chief cornerstone.
This is the LORD's doing;
  it is marvelous in our eyes.
This is the day that the LORD has made;
  let us rejoice and be glad in it.
Save us, we beseech you, O LORD!
  O LORD, we beseech you, give us success!

Side 1:
Blessed is the one who comes in the name of the LORD.
  We bless you from the house of the LORD.
The LORD is God,
  and he has given us light.
Bind the festal procession with branches,
  up to the horns of the altar.

Side 2:
You are my God, and I will give thanks to you;
  you are my God, I will extol you.

O give thanks to the LORD, for he is good,
  for his steadfast love endures forever.

All pause for a moment of silence. The minister motions for the assembly to stand and all proclaim together:

All:

Glory to the Father, and to the Son, and to the
  Holy Spirit,
As it was in the beginning, is now
    and will be for ever. Amen.

The assembly may be seated.

Reading from the Word of God

One of the following selections from the Holy Gospels may be proclaimed. The assembly is invited to stand. Other scripture selections that may be used are found on pages 21–30. If a Gospel isn't selected, the assembly should remain seated.

Matthew 5:1–12

When Jesus saw the crowds, he went up the mountain; and after he sat down, his disciples came to him. Then he began to speak, and taught them, saying:

"Blessed are the poor in spirit, for theirs is the kingdom of heaven.

"Blessed are those who mourn, for they will be comforted.

"Blessed are the meek, for they will inherit the earth.

"Blessed are those who hunger and thirst for righteousness, for they will be filled.

"Blessed are the merciful, for they will receive mercy.

"Blessed are the pure in heart, for they will see God.

"Blessed are the peacemakers, for they will be called children of God.

"Blessed are those who are persecuted for righteousness' sake, for theirs is the kingdom of heaven.

"Blessed are you when people revile you and persecute you and utter all kinds of evil against you falsely on my account. Rejoice and be glad, for your reward is great in heaven, for in the same way they persecuted the prophets who were before you."

Mark 4:26–32

[Jesus] said, "The kingdom of God is as if someone would scatter seed on the ground, and would sleep and rise night and day, and the seed would sprout and grow, he does not know how. The earth produces of itself, first the stalk, then the head, then the full grain in the head. But when the grain is ripe, at once he goes in with his sickle, because the harvest has come."

He also said, "With what can we compare the kingdom of God, or what parable will we use for it? It is like a mustard seed, which, when sown upon the ground, is the smallest of all the seeds on earth; yet when it is sown it grows up and becomes the greatest of all shrubs, and puts forth large branches, so that the birds of the air can make nests in its shade."

Sermon/Reflection

The assembly may be seated for the sermon/reflection.

After the sermon or reflection all pause for a moment of silent prayer.

Song of Praise

Music selections are found on pages 58–74.

Prayer of the Faithful

A reader may be chosen to offer these or similar prayers. The assembly may stand.

Prayer leader:

Let us pray to the God of heaven and earth,
who reveals to [us] the mysteries of the kingdom.

Reader:

May pastors and all Christians pattern their lives after
the example of the Master, who came in humility and
called to himself the childlike of heart.

We pray to the Lord:

All: Lord, hear our prayer.

Reader:

May leaders and citizens work to banish the weapons
of war, so that a new dominion of peace may reach
to the ends of the earth.

We pray to the Lord:

All: Lord, hear our prayer.

Reader:

May those weary in body, mind or spirit find in Christ
the rest they long for and in Christ's disciples the
assistance they need.

We pray to the Lord:

All: Lord, hear our prayer.

Reader:
For those who travel, may they see God's handiwork in the splendor of wind and sea, and be renewed in spirit by their time of recreation.

We pray to the Lord:

All: Lord, hear our prayer.

Reader:
For the travelers among us, may they experience the enriching gift of hospitality.
We pray to the Lord:

All: Lord, hear our prayer.

Reader:
May all who bear the yoke of illness or the burden of pain come to know Christ in the support we all offer one another.

We pray to the Lord:

All: Lord, hear our prayer.

Reader:
May the Spirit of God who raised Jesus from the dead raise our dead and give them eternal life.

We pray to the Lord:

All: Lord, hear our prayer.

The Lord's Prayer

Prayer leader:
Let us pray for the coming of the kingdom as Jesus
taught us:

All:
Our Father, who art in heaven,
hallowed be thy name;
thy kingdom come;
thy will be done on earth as it is in heaven.
Give us this day our daily bread;
and forgive us our trespasses
as we forgive those who trespass against us;
and lead us not into temptation,
but deliver us from evil.
For the kingdom, the power and the glory are yours,
 now and for ever.

All: Amen.

Sign of Peace

Prayer leader:
As one body in Christ, let us offer to one another
a sign of peace.

The assembly offers a sign of peace to those standing nearby.

Prayer of Blessing

Prayer leader:
Let us pray:

Allow a moment of silent prayer.

All-powerful and ever-living God,
when Abraham left his own land
and departed from his own people,
you kept him safe all through his journey.
Protect us, who also are your servants:
walk by our side to help us;
be our companion and our strength on the road
and our refuge in every adversity.
Lead us, O Lord,
so that we will reach our destination in safety
and happily return to our homes.

We ask this through Christ our Lord.

All: Amen.

DISMISSAL

Prayer leader:
Let us go forth in the peace of Christ.

All: Thanks be to God!

Closing Hymn

Music selections are found on pages 58–74.

Scripture Selections for Ecumenical Prayer Services

The minister may choose any of the following selections from scripture:

Old Testament

Deuteronomy 7:7–11

It was not because you were more numerous than any other people that the LORD set his heart on you and chose you—for you were the fewest of all peoples. It was because the LORD loved you and kept the oath that he swore to your ancestors, that the LORD has brought you out with a mighty hand, and redeemed you from the house of slavery, from the hand of Pharaoh king of Egypt. Know therefore that the LORD your God is God, the faithful God who maintains covenant loyalty with those who love him and keep his commandments, to a thousand generations, and who repays in their own person those who reject him. He does not delay but repays in their own person those who reject him. Therefore, observe diligently the commandment—the statutes, and the ordinances—that I am commanding you today.

Isaiah 56:1, 6–7

Thus says the LORD:
Maintain justice, and do what is right,
for soon my salvation will come,
  and my deliverance be revealed.

And the foreigners who join themselves to the LORD,
    to minister to him, to love the name of the LORD,
        and to be his servants,
all who keep the sabbath, and do not profane it,
    and hold fast my covenant—
these I will bring to my holy mountain,
    and make them joyful in my house of prayer;
their burnt offerings and their sacrifices
    will be accepted on my altar;
for my house shall be called a house of prayer
    for all peoples.

Isaiah 35:5–7a

[Thus, says the Lord:]
Then the eyes of the blind shall be opened,
    and the ears of the deaf unstopped;
then the lame shall leap like a deer,
    and the tongue of the speechless sing for joy.
For waters shall break forth in the wilderness,
    and streams in the desert;
the burning sand shall become a pool,
    and the thirsty ground springs of water.

PSALMS

Psalm 95

O come, let us sing to the LORD; let us make a joyful
    noise to the rock of our salvation!
Let us come into his presence with thanksgiving;
    let us make a joyful noise to him with songs
        of praise!

For the LORD is a great God,
    and a great King above all gods.
In his hand are the depths of the earth;
    the heights of the mountains are his also.
The sea is his, for he made it,
    and the dry land, which his hands have formed.

O come, let us worship and bow down,
    let us kneel before the LORD, our Maker!
For he is our God,
    and we are the people of his pasture,
    and the sheep of his hand.

O that today you would listen to his voice!
    Do not harden your hearts, as at Meribah,
    as on the day at Massah in the wilderness,
when your ancestors tested me,
    and put me to the proof, though they had seen
        my work.
For forty years I loathed that generation
    and said, "They are a people whose hearts go astray,
    and they do not regard my ways."
Therefore in my anger I swore,
    "They shall not enter my rest."

Psalm 98
O sing to the LORD a new song,
    for he has done marvelous things.
His right hand and his holy arm
    have gotten him victory.

The LORD has made known his victory;
 he has revealed his vindication in the sight of
  the nations.
He has remembered his steadfast love and faithfulness
 to the house of Israel.
All the ends of the earth have seen
 the victory of our God.

Make a joyful noise to the LORD, all the earth;
 break forth into joyous song and sing praises.
Sing praises to the LORD with the lyre,
 with the lyre and the sound of melody.
With trumpets and the sound of the horn
 make a joyful noise before the King, the LORD.

Let the sea roar, and all that fills it;
 the world and those who live in it.
Let the floods clap their hands;
 let the hills sing together for joy
at the presence of the LORD, for he is coming
 to judge the earth.
He will judge the world with righteousness,
 and the peoples with equity.

Psalm 117

Praise the LORD, all you nations!
 Extol him, all you peoples!
For great is his steadfast love toward us,
 and the faithfulness of the LORD endures forever.
Praise the LORD!

New Testament

Acts of the Apostles 2:42–47

They devoted themselves to the apostles' teaching and fellowship, to the breaking of bread and the prayers.

Awe came upon everyone, because many wonders and signs were being done by the apostles. All who believed were together and had all things in common; they would sell their possessions and goods and distribute the proceeds to all, as any had need. Day by day, as they spent much time together in the temple, they broke bread at home and ate their food with glad and generous hearts, praising God and having the goodwill of all the people. And day by day the Lord added to their number those who were being saved.

Ephesians 4:1–6

I therefore, the prisoner in the Lord, beg you to lead a life worthy of the calling to which you have been called, with all humility and gentleness, with patience, bearing with one another in love, making every effort to maintain the unity of the Spirit in the bond of peace. There is one body and one Spirit, just as you were called to the one hope of your calling, one Lord, one faith, one baptism, one God and Father of all, who is above all and through all and in all.

Romans 6:3–11

Do you not know that all of us who have been baptized into Christ Jesus were baptized into his death? Therefore we have been buried with him by baptism into death, so that, just as Christ was raised from the dead by the glory of the Father, so we too might walk in newness of life.

For if we have been united with him in a death like his, we will certainly be united with him in a resurrection like his. We know that our old self was crucified with him so that the body of sin might be destroyed, and we might no longer be enslaved to sin. For whoever has died is freed from sin. But if we have died with Christ, we believe that we will also live with him. We know that Christ, being raised from the dead, will never die again; death no longer has dominion over him. The death he died, he died to sin, once for all; but the life he lives, he lives to God. So you also must consider yourselves dead to sin and alive to God in Christ Jesus.

Galatians 3:19–29

Why then the law? It was added because of transgressions, until the offspring would come to whom the promise had been made; and it was ordained through angels by a mediator. Now a mediator involves more than one party; but God is one.

Is the law then opposed to the promises of God? Certainly not! For if a law had been given that could make alive, then righteousness would indeed come through the law. But the scripture has imprisoned all things under the power of sin, so that what was promised through faith in Jesus Christ might be given to those who believe.

Now before faith came, we were imprisoned and guarded under the law until faith would be revealed. Therefore the law was our disciplinarian until Christ came, so that we might be justified by faith. But now that faith has come, we are no longer subject to a disciplinarian, for in Christ Jesus you are all children of God through faith. As many of you as were baptized into Christ have clothed yourselves with Christ. There is no longer Jew or Greek, there is no longer slave or free, there is no longer male and female; for all of you are one in Christ Jesus. And if you belong to Christ, then you are Abraham's offspring, heirs according to the promise.

GOSPEL

Matthew 5:13–16

"You are the salt of the earth; but if salt has lost its taste, how can its saltiness be restored? It is no longer good for anything, but is thrown out and trampled under foot.

"You are the light of the world. A city built on a hill cannot be hid. No one after lighting a lamp puts it under the bushel basket, but on the lampstand, and it gives light to all in the house. In the same way, let your light shine before others, so that they may see your good works and give glory to your Father in heaven.

Matthew 16:24–28

Then Jesus told his disciples, "If any want to become my followers, let them deny themselves and take up their cross and follow me. For those who want to save their life will lose it, and those who lose their life for my sake will find it. For what will it profit them if they gain the whole world but forfeit their life? Or what will they give in return for their life?

"For the Son of Man is to come with his angels in the glory of his Father, and then he will repay every-one for what has been done. Truly I tell you, there are some standing here who will not taste death before they see the Son of Man coming in his kingdom."

Mark 9:2–8

Six days later, Jesus took with him Peter and James and John, and led them up a high mountain apart, by themselves. And he was transfigured before them, and his clothes became dazzling white, such as no one on earth could bleach them. And there appeared to them Elijah with Moses, who were talking with Jesus. Then Peter said to Jesus, "Rabbi, it is good for us to be here; let us make three dwellings, one for you, one for Moses, and one for Elijah." He did not know what to say, for they were terrified. Then a cloud overshadowed them, and from the cloud there came a voice, "This is my Son, the Beloved; listen to him!" Suddenly when they looked around, they saw no one with them any more, but only Jesus.

Luke 6:27–36

"But I say to you that listen, Love your enemies, do good to those who hate you, bless those who curse you, pray for those who abuse you. If anyone strikes you on the cheek, offer the other also; and from anyone who takes away your coat do not withhold even your shirt. Give to everyone who begs from you; and if anyone takes away your goods, do not ask for them again. Do to others as you would have them do to you.

"If you love those who love you, what credit is that to you? For even sinners love those who love them. If you do good to those who do good to you, what credit is that to you? For even sinners do the same. If you lend to those from whom you hope to receive, what credit is that to you? Even sinners lend to sinners, to receive as much again. But love your enemies, do good, and lend, expecting nothing in return. Your reward will be great, and you will be children of the Most High; for he is kind to the ungrateful and the wicked. Be merciful, just as your Father is merciful.

John 1:1–5

In the beginning was the Word, and the Word was with God, and the Word was God. He was in the beginning with God. All things came into being through him, and without him not one thing came into being. What has come into being in him was life, and the life was the light of all people. The light shines in the darkness, and the darkness did not overcome it.

John 3:16–21

"For God so loved the world that he gave his only Son, so that everyone who believes in him may not perish but may have eternal life.

"Indeed, God did not send the Son into the world to condemn the world, but in order that the world might be saved through him. Those who believe in him are not condemned; but those who do not believe are condemned already, because they have not believed in the name of the only Son of God. And this is the judgment, that the light has come into the world, and people loved darkness rather than light because their deeds were evil. For all who do evil hate the light and do not come to the light, so that their deeds may not be exposed. But those who do what is true come to the light, so that it may be clearly seen that their deeds have been done in God."

INTERRELIGIOUS SERVICE

CALL TO GATHER

Opening Hymn

> *All stand for the Opening Hymn. Music selections are found on pages 58–74.*

Service Leader:

In the name of our loving Creator, we give thanks and praise.

All: Let us bless the Source of Life!

Words of Welcome

> *The minister welcomes those present and provides an introductory comment regarding the nature of the service.*

Opening Meditation

Service leader:

Let us pause

> *Allow a moment of silence.*

In you, Lord our God,
all things have their beginning, continuation, and end.
Grace us with your saving presence,
aid us with your constant help
and let us glorify you,
now and for ever.

All: Amen.

MEDITATIONS

Readers may be selected to read one or more of the following meditations. A moment of silence should follow each meditation. The assembly is seated.

Option A

Psalm 8

O LORD, our Sovereign,
  how majestic is your name in all the earth!
You have set your glory above the heavens.
  Out of the mouths of babes and infants
you have founded a bulwark because of your foes,
  to silence the enemy and the avenger.

When I look at your heavens, the work of your fingers,
  the moon and the stars that you have established;
what are human beings that you are mindful of them,
  mortals that you care for them?

Yet you have made them a little lower than God,
  and crowned them with glory and honor.
You have given them dominion over the works of
    your hands;
  you have put all things under their feet,
all sheep and oxen,
  and also the beasts of the field,
the birds of the air, and the fish of the sea,
  whatever passes along the paths of the seas.
O LORD, our Sovereign,
  how majestic is your name in all the earth!

Option B

Song of Solomon 1:2–17

Let him kiss me with the kisses of his mouth!
For your love is better than wine,
   your anointing oils are fragrant,
your name is perfume poured out;
   therefore the maidens love you.
Draw me after you, let us make haste.
   The king has brought me into his chambers.
We will exult and rejoice in you;
   we will extol your love more than wine;
   rightly do they love you.

I am black and beautiful,
   O daughters of Jerusalem,
like the tents of Kedar,
   like the curtains of Solomon.
Do not gaze at me because I am dark,
   because the sun has gazed on me.
My mother's sons were angry with me;
   they made me keeper of the vineyards,
   but my own vineyard I have not kept!
Tell me, you whom my soul loves,
   where you pasture your flock,
   where you make it lie down at noon;
for why should I be like one who is veiled
   beside the flocks of your companions?

If you do not know,
   O fairest among women,
follow the tracks of the flock,
   and pasture your kids
   beside the shepherds' tents.

I compare you, my love,
   to a mare among Pharaoh's chariots.
Your cheeks are comely with ornaments,
   your neck with strings of jewels.
We will make you ornaments of gold,
   studded with silver.

While the king was on his couch,
   my nard gave forth its fragrance.
My beloved is to me a bag of myrrh
   that lies between my breasts.
My beloved is to me a cluster of henna blossoms
   in the vineyards of En-gedi.

Ah, you are beautiful, my love;
   ah, you are beautiful;
   your eyes are doves.
Ah, you are beautiful, my beloved,
   truly lovely.
Our couch is green;
   the beams of our house are cedar,
   our rafters are pine.

Option C

Koran 87.1–87.17

Glorify the name of your Lord, the Most High,
Who creates, then makes complete,
And Who makes (things) according to a measure,
     then guides (them to their goal),
And Who brings forth herbage,
Then makes it dried up, dust-colored.
We will make you recite so you shall not forget,
Except what Allah pleases, surely He knows the
     manifest, and what is hidden.
And We will make your way smooth to a state of ease.
Therefore do remind, surely reminding does profit.
He who fears will mind,
And the most unfortunate one will avoid it,
Who shall enter the great fire;
Then therein he shall neither live nor die.
He indeed shall be successful who purifies himself,
And magnifies the name of his Lord and prays.
Nay! you prefer the life of this world,
While the hereafter is better and more lasting.

Moment of Silence

Song of Praise

Music selections are found on pages 58–74.

Petitions

All stand for the Petitions.

We come before our Divine Master with petitions for the needs of the world.

Reader:

For all to be an instrument of peace:

All: Loving Creator, hear us.

Reader:

For the sowing of love in the face of hatred:

All: Loving Creator, hear us.

Reader:

For pardon for the injured:
Loving Creator, hear us.

Reader:

For the light of faith to illumine the darkness of doubt:

All: Loving Creator, hear us.

Reader:

For hope and joy to embrace those who despair:

All: Loving God, hear us.

O, Divine Master,
Hear the needs of those before you,
and grant that we may not so much seek to be consoled
    as to console;
to be understood, as to understand;
and to be loved, as to love;
for it is in giving that we receive,
it is in pardoning that we are pardoned,

and it is in dying that we are born to eternal life.
We ask these things through our Creator.

All: Amen.

DISMISSAL

Service Leader:

May the Lord bless you and keep you.
May his face shine upon you and be gracious to you.
May he look upon you with kindness and give you
his peace.

All: Amen.

Closing Hymn

Music selections are found on pages 58–74.

RENEWAL OF CHRISTIAN MARRIAGE VOWS
OPTION A

CALL TO WORSHIP

Opening Hymn

Music selections are found on pages 58–74.

Prayer leader:

In the name of the Father, and of the Son, and of the Holy Spirit.

All: Amen.

Prayer leader:

Grace to you and peace from God our Father and the Lord Jesus Christ our bridegroom.

All: And also with you.

The minister should welcome and prepare the couple and the assembly for the renewal of marriage vows.

Opening Prayer

Prayer leader:

Let us pray:

Allow a moment of silent prayer.

God our Father,
you created man and woman
to love each other
in the bond of marriage.

Bless and strengthen N. and N.
May their marriage become an increasingly more
    perfect sign
of the union between Christ and his Church.

We ask this through our Lord Jesus Christ, your Son,
who lives and reigns with you and the Holy Spirit,
one God, for ever and ever.

All: Amen.

READING OF THE WORD OF GOD

Scripture selections are found on pages 49–57.

Sermon/Reflection

The minister gives a sermon or reflection regarding the marriage renewal and biblical texts.

The couple are invited to pray in silence before they renew their marriage vows.

RENEWAL OF MARRIAGE VOWS

The couple renew their marriage vows as the minister proclaims the following prayer:

Prayer leader:
Lord of hope and promise,
N. and N. come before you
to renew their marital covenant.
Bless their lives and their love
and continue to strengthen their commitment to
    one another.

May their union be a witness and example
of the love of Christ for his people,
through whom we make our prayer.

All: Amen.

PRAYER OF THE FAITHFUL

A reader says the following or similar prayers:

Prayer leader:
God has called us to relationship through the covenant
of marriage. Let us bring our needs before him.

Reader:
For the Church, may her members be faithful to the
grace of God.

We pray to the Lord:

All: Lord, renew the covenant of love!

Reader:
For those who are married, may they be a sign and
witness to Christ's salvific love.

We pray to the Lord:

All: Lord, renew the covenant of love!

Reader:
For those who are celebrating their (10th, 20th, 25th,
50th) wedding anniversaries, may they recommit their
lives to Christ, our bridegroom.

We pray to the Lord:

All: Lord, renew the covenant of love!

Reader:

For those whose unions are tested and strained, may they be filled with the spirit of God and strengthened in fidelity.

We pray to the Lord:

All: Lord, renew the covenant of love!

PRAYER OF BLESSING

The minister blesses the couple with the following prayer:

Lord, God and Creator,
we bless and praise your name.
In the beginning you made man and woman,
so that they might enter a communion of life and love.
You likewise blessed the union of N. with N.,
so that they might reflect the union of Christ with
    his Church:
look with kindness on them today.
Amid the joys and struggles of their life
you have preserved the union between them;
renew their marriage covenant,
increase your love in them,
and strengthen their bond of peace,
so that (surrounded by their children)
they may always rejoice in the gift of your blessing.

We ask this through Christ our Lord.

All: Amen.

In some circumstances it may be fitting to add a song of praise following the Prayer of Blessing. Music selections are found on pages 54–78.

DISMISSAL

Prayer leader:
May God, the almighty Father,
continue to foster undivided unity.

All: Amen.

Prayer leader:
May the only Son of God bring you peace
and strengthen you in fidelity.

All: Amen.

Prayer leader:
May the Holy Spirit
ignite your hearts with love, respect, and compassion.

All: Amen.

Prayer leader:
And may our loving God bless your union,
in the name of the Father,
and the Son, and the Holy Spirit.
Amen.

Prayer leader:
Let us go forth in the peace of Christ.

All: Thanks be to God!

Closing Hymn

Music selections are found on pages 54–78.

Renewal of Christian Marriage Vows
Option B

Call to Worship

Prayer leader:
In the name of the Father, and of the Son,
and of the Holy Spirit.

All: Amen.

Prayer leader:
Grace to you and peace from God our Father and the
Lord Jesus Christ our bridegroom.

All: And also with you.

*The minister should welcome and prepare the couple and the
assembly for the renewal of marriage vows.*

Opening Prayer

Prayer leader:
Let us pray:

Allow a moment of silent prayer.

God our Father,
you created man and woman
to love each other
in the bond of marriage.
Bless and strengthen N. and N.
May their marriage become an increasingly more
	perfect sign
of the union between Christ and his Church.

We ask this through our Lord Jesus Christ, your Son,
who lives and reigns with you and the Holy Spirit,
one God, for ever and ever.

All: Amen.

READING FROM THE WORD OF GOD

*These or similar short readings may be read. Other scripture
selections are found on pages 49–57.*

Matthew 22:37

[Jesus] said to him, "You shall love the Lord your God
with all your heart, and with all your soul, and with all
your mind."

Mark 10:6–9

But from the beginning of creation, "God made them
male and female." "For this reason a man shall leave his
father and mother and be joined to his wife, and the
two shall become one flesh." So they are no longer two,
but one flesh. Therefore what God has joined together,
let no one separate.

John 15:9–11

[Jesus said:] "As the Father has loved me, so I have
loved you; abide in my love. If you keep my commandments, you will abide in my love, just as I have kept
my Father's commandments and abide in his love.
I have said these things to you so that my joy may be
in you, and that your joy may be complete."

Renewal of Marriage Vows

Pric of Blessing

Prayer of Blessing

The couple renew their marriage vows as the minister proclaims the following prayer:

Lord God and Creator,
we bless and praise your name.
In the beginning you made man and woman,
so that they might enter a communion of life and love.
You likewise blessed the union of N. with N.,
so that they might reflect the union of Christ with
    his Church:
look with kindness on them today.
Amid the joys and struggles of their life
you have preserved the union between them;
renew their marriage covenant,
increase your love in them,
and strengthen their bond of peace,
So that (surrounded by their children)
they may always rejoice in the gift of your blessing.

We ask this through Christ our Lord.

All: Amen.

Dismissal

Prayer leader:
May God, the almighty Father,
continue to foster undivided unity in your married lives.

All: Amen.

Prayer leader:
May the only Son of God bring you peace
and strengthen you in your covenant.

All: Amen.

Prayer leader:
May the Holy Spirit
ignite your hearts with love, respect, and compassion.

All: Amen.

Prayer leader:
And may our loving God bless your union,
in the name of the Father,
and the Son, and the Holy Spirit.

All: Amen.

Prayer leader:
Let us go forth in the peace of Christ.

All: Thanks be to God!

Scripture selections for the Renewal of Christian Marriage Vows

Old Testament

Genesis 2:18–24

Then the LORD God said, "It is not good that the man should be alone; I will make him a helper as his partner." So out of the ground the LORD God formed every animal of the field and every bird of the air, and brought them to the man to see what he would call them; and whatever the man called every living creature, that was its name. The man gave names to all cattle, and to the birds of the air, and to every animal of the field; but for the man there was not found a helper as his partner. So the LORD God caused a deep sleep to fall upon the man, and he slept; then he took one of his ribs and closed up its place with flesh. And the rib that the LORD God had taken from the man he made into a woman and brought her to the man. Then the man said, "This at last is bone of my bones and flesh of my flesh; this one shall be called Woman, for out of Man this one was taken." Therefore a man leaves his father and his mother and clings to his wife, and they become one flesh.

Song of Solomon 2:1–13

I am a rose of Sharon,
    a lily of the valleys.

As a lily among brambles,
    so is my love among maidens.

As an apple tree among the trees of the wood,
    so is my beloved among young men.
With great delight I sat in his shadow,
    and his fruit was sweet to my taste.
He brought me to the banqueting house,
    and his intention toward me was love.
Sustain me with raisins,
    refresh me with apples;
    for I am faint with love.
O that his left hand were under my head,
    and that his right hand embraced me!
I adjure you, O daughters of Jerusalem,
    by the gazelles or the wild does:
do not stir up or awaken love until it is ready!

The voice of my beloved!
    Look, he comes,
leaping upon the mountains,
    bounding over the hills.
My beloved is like a gazelle
    or a young stag.
Look, there he stands
    behind our wall,
gazing in at the windows,
    looking through the lattice.

My beloved speaks and says to me:
"Arise, my love, my fair one,
    and come away;
for now the winter is past,
    the rain is over and gone.
The flowers appear on the earth;
    the time of singing has come,
and the voice of the turtledove
    is heard in our land.
The fig tree puts forth its figs,
    and the vines are in blossom;
    they give forth fragrance.
Arise, my love, my fair one,
    and come away.

Jeremiah 31:31–34

The days are surely coming, says the LORD, when
I will make a new covenant with the house of Israel
and the house of Judah. It will not be like the covenant that I made with their ancestors when I took them
by the hand to bring them out of the land of Egypt—
a covenant that they broke, though I was their husband,
says the LORD. But this is the covenant that I will
make with the house of Israel after those days, says the
LORD: I will put my law within them, and I will write
it on their hearts; and I will be their God, and they shall
be my people. No longer shall they teach one another,
or say to each other, "Know the LORD," for they shall
all know me, from the least of them to the greatest, says
the LORD; for I will forgive their iniquity, and remember their sin no more.

PSALMS

Psalm 103:1–2, 8, 13, 17–18a

Bless the LORD, O my soul,
   and all that is within me,
    bless his holy name.
Bless the LORD, O my soul,
   and do not forget all his benefits—

The LORD is merciful and gracious,
   slow to anger and abounding in steadfast love.
As a father has compassion for his children,
   so the LORD has compassion for those who fear him.

But the steadfast love of the LORD is from everlasting
    to everlasting
   on those who fear him,
   and his righteousness to children's children,
to those who keep his covenant
   and remember to do his commandments.

Psalm 128:1–5

Happy is everyone who fears the LORD,
   who walks in his ways.
You shall eat the fruit of the labor of your hands;
   you shall be happy, and it shall go well with you.

Your wife will be like a fruitful vine
   within your house;
your children will be like olive shoots
   around your table.
Thus shall the man be blessed
   who fears the LORD.

The LORD bless you from Zion.
May you see the prosperity of Jerusalem
all the days of your life.

Psalm 145:8–10, 15, 17–18

The LORD is gracious and merciful,
slow to anger and abounding in steadfast love.
The LORD is good to all,
and his compassion is over all that he has made.

All your works shall give thanks to you, O LORD,
and all your faithful shall bless you.

The eyes of all look to you,
and you give them their food in due season.
The LORD is just in all his ways,
and kind in all his doings.
The LORD is near to all who call on him,
to all who call on him in truth.

NEW TESTAMENT

1 Corinthians 13

If I speak in the tongues of mortals and of angels,
but do not have love, I am a noisy gong or a clanging
cymbal. And if I have prophetic powers, and understand all mysteries and all knowledge, and if I have all
faith, so as to remove mountains, but do not have love,
I am nothing. If I give away all my possessions, and
if I hand over my body so that I may boast, but do not
have love, I gain nothing.

Love is patient; love is kind; love is not envious
or boastful or arrogant or rude. It does not insist

on its own way; it is not irritable or resentful; it does not rejoice in wrongdoing, but rejoices in the truth. It bears all things, believes all things, hopes all things, endures all things.

Love never ends. But as for prophecies, they will come to an end; as for tongues, they will cease; as for knowledge, it will come to an end. For we know only in part, and we prophesy only in part; but when the complete comes, the partial will come to an end. When I was a child, I spoke like a child, I thought like a child, I reasoned like a child; when I became an adult, I put an end to childish ways. For now we see in a mirror, dimly, but then we will see face to face. Now I know only in part; then I will know fully, even as I have been fully known. And now faith, hope, and love abide, these three; and the greatest of these is love.

Ephesians 5:1–2, 22–33

Therefore be imitators of God, as beloved children, and live in love, as Christ loved us and gave himself up for us, a fragrant offering and sacrifice to God.

Wives, be subject to your husbands as you are to the Lord. For the husband is the head of the wife just as Christ is the head of the church, the body of which he is the Savior. Just as the church is subject to Christ, so also wives ought to be, in everything, to their husbands.

Husbands, love your wives, just as Christ loved the church and gave himself up for her, in order to make her holy by cleansing her with the washing of water by the word, so as to present the church to himself in splendor, without a spot or wrinkle or anything of the kind—yes, so that she may be holy and without blemish. In the same way, husbands should love their wives as they do their own bodies. He who loves his wife loves himself. For no one ever hates his own body, but he nourishes and tenderly cares for it, just as Christ does for the church, because we are members of his body. "For this reason a man will leave his father and mother and be joined to his wife, and the two will become one flesh." This is a great mystery, and I am applying it to Christ and the church. Each of you, however, should love his wife as himself, and a wife should respect her husband.

1 John 4:7–13

Beloved, let us love one another, because love is from God; everyone who loves is born of God and knows God. Whoever does not love does not know God, for God is love. God's love was revealed among us in this way: God sent his only Son into the world so that we might live through him. In this is love, not that we loved God but that he loved us and sent his Son to be the atoning sacrifice for our sins. Beloved, since God loved us so much, we also ought to love one another. No one has ever seen God; if we love one another, God lives in us, and his love is perfected in us.

By this we know that we abide in him and he in us, because he has given us of his Spirit.

GOSPEL

Mark 10:6–9

But from the beginning of creation, "God made them male and female." "For this reason a man shall leave his father and mother and be joined to his wife, and the two shall become one flesh." So they are no longer two, but one flesh. Therefore what God has joined together, let no one separate.

John 2:1–11

On the third day there was a wedding in Cana of Galilee, and the mother of Jesus was there. Jesus and his disciples had also been invited to the wedding. When the wine gave out, the mother of Jesus said to him, "They have no wine." And Jesus said to her, "Woman, what concern is that to you and to me? My hour has not yet come." His mother said to the servants, "Do whatever he tells you." Now standing there were six stone water jars for the Jewish rites of purification, each holding twenty or thirty gallons. Jesus said to them, "Fill the jars with water." And they filled them up to the brim. He said to them, "Now draw some out, and take it to the chief steward." So they took it. When the steward tasted the water that had become wine, and did not dfknow where it came from (though the servants who had drawn the water knew), the steward called the bridegroom and said to him, "Everyone serves the good wine first, and then the inferior wine after the guests have become drunk. But you have kept the good wine until now." Jesus did this, the first of his signs, in Cana of Galilee, and revealed his glory; and his disciples believed in him.

John 15:9–16

As the Father has loved me, so I have loved you; abide in my love. If you keep my commandments, you will abide in my love, just as I have kept my Father's commandments and abide in his love. I have said these things to you so that my joy may be in you, and that your joy may be complete.

This is my commandment, that you love one another as I have loved you. No one has greater love than this, to lay down one's life for one's friends. You are my friends if you do what I command you. I do not call you servants any longer, because the servant does not know what the master is doing; but I have called you friends, because I have made known to you everything that I have heard from my Father. You did not choose me but I chose you. And I appointed you to go and bear fruit, fruit that will last, so that the Father will give you whatever you ask him in my name.

Amazing Grace

1. A - maz - ing grace! how sweet the sound,
2. 'Twas grace that taught my heart to fear,
3. The Lord has prom - ised good to me,
4. Through man - y dan - gers, toils, and snares,
5. When we've been there ten thou - sand years,

That saved a wretch like me!
And grace my fears re - lieved;
His word my hope se - cures;
I have al - read - y come;
Bright shin - ing as the sun,

I once was lost, but now am found,
How pre - cious did that grace ap - pear
He will my shield and por - tion be
'Tis grace has brought me safe thus far,
We've no less days to sing God's praise

Was blind, but now I see.
The hour I first be - lieved!
As long as life en - dures.
And grace will lead me home.
Than when we'd first be - gun.

Text: St. 1-4 John Newton, 1725-1807; St. 5 ascr. to John Rees, fl. 1859
Tune: NEW BRITAIN, CM; *Virginia Harmony;* 1831

Come, Now Almighty King

1. Come, now al - might - y King, Help us your
2. Come, now In - car - nate Son, Your life in
3. Come, ho - ly Com - fort - er, Your sa - cred
4. To the great One in Three E - ter - nal

name to sing, Help us to praise.
us be - gun, Our prayer at - tend.
wit - ness bear In this glad hour.
prais - es be For ev - er more!

Fa - ther all glo - ri - ous, Ev - er vic - to - ri - ous,
Come and your peo - ple bless And give your Word suc - cess;
Your grace to us im - part, Now rule in ev - 'ry heart
Your sov - 'reign maj - es - ty May we in glo - ry see

Come and reign o - ver us, An - cient of Days.
Strength-en your right - eous - ness, Sav - ior and Friend!
Nev - er from us de - part, Spir - it of Pow'r!
And to e - ter - ni - ty Love and a - dore!

Text: Anon. c.1757
Tune: ITALIAN HYMN, 66 4 666 4; Felice De Giardini, 1716-1796

Come, O thou Traveler Unknown

1. Come, O thou Trav-el-er un-known, whom still I hold, but can-not see! My com-pa-ny be-fore is gone, and I am left a-lone with thee; with thee all night I mean to stay and wres-tle till the break of day.

2. I need not tell thee who I am, my mis-er-y and sin de-clare; thy-self hast called me by my name, look on thy hands and read it there. But who, I ask thee, who art thou? Tell me thy name, and tell me now.

3. Yield to me now, for I am weak but con-fi-dent in self-de-spair! Speak to my heart, in bless-ing speak, be con-quered by my in-stant prayer; speak, or thou nev-er hence shalt move, and tell me if thy name is Love.

4. 'Tis Love! 'tis Love! thou diedst for me! I hear thy whis-per in my heart; the morn-ing breaks, the shad-ows flee, pure U-ni-ver-sal Love thou art; to me, to all, thy mer-cies move: thy na-ture and thy name is Love.

5. Lame as I am, I'll run my race, hell, death, and sin by faith o'er-come; I'll leap for joy, and as a bound-ing hart fly home, through all e-ter-ni-ty to prove thy na-ture and thy name is Love.

Text: "Wrestling Jacob," Charles Wesley, 1739
Tune: ST. CATHERINE, LM Henry F. Hemy, 1818-1888; Adapt. by James. G. Walton, 1821-1905

60

Come, Ye Thankful People, Come

1. Come, ye thank-ful   peo-ple, come, Raise the song of   har-vest home:
2. All   the world is   God's own field, Fruit un - to his   praise to   yield;
3. For   the Lord our   God shall come, And shall take this   har-vest home;
4. Ev - en   so, Lord, quick-ly   come To your fi - nal   har-vest home;

All   is   safe-ly   gath-ered   in, Ere the win-ter   storms be - gin;
Wheat and tares to - geth - er   sown, Un - to   joy or   sor - row grown:
From this field shall   in   that   day All   of - fens - es   purge   a - way;
Gath - er   all your   peo - ple   in, Free from sor-row,   free   from   sin;

God,   our Mak - er,   does pro - vide For our   wants to   be   sup - plied;
First   the blade, and   then the   ear, Then the   full   corn   shall   ap - pear:
Give   the an - gels   charge at   last In   the   fire   the   tares   to   cast,
There, for - ev - er   pur - i - fied, In your   pres - ence   to   a - bide;

Come   to God's own   tem - ple, come, Raise   the   song   of   har-vest home.
Grant,   O   har - vest Lord, that   we Whole-some grain and   pure may   be.
But   the fruit - ful   ears   to   store   In   his   gar - ner   ev - er - more.
Come with all your   an - gels, come, Raise   the   glo - rious   har-vest home.

Text: Henry Alford, 1810-1871, alt.
Tune: ST. GEORGE'S WINDSOR, 77 77 D; George J. Elvey, 1816-1893

Crown Him with Many Crowns

1. Crown him with man - y crowns, The Lamb up - on his throne;
2. Crown him the Lord of life, Who tri - umphed o'er the grave,
3. Crown him the Lord of love, Be - hold his hands and side,
4. Crown him the Lord of peace, Whose power a scep - ter sways
5. Crown him the Lord of years, The ris - en Lord sub - lime,

Hark! how the heaven-ly an - them drowns All mu - sic but its own.
And rose vic - to - rious in the strife For those he came to save.
Rich wounds yet vis - i - ble a - bove In beau - ty glo - ri - fied.
From pole to pole, that wars may cease, Ab - sorbed in prayer and praise.
Cre - a - tor of the roll - ing spheres, The Mas - ter of all time.

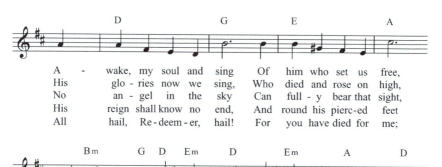

A - wake, my soul and sing Of him who set us free,
His glo - ries now we sing, Who died and rose on high,
No an - gel in the sky Can full - y bear that sight,
His reign shall know no end, And round his pierc-ed feet
All hail, Re - deem - er, hail! For you have died for me;

And hail him as your heav'n-ly King Through all e - ter - ni - ty.
Who died, e - ter - nal life to bring, And lives that death may die.
But down-ward bends his burn-ing eye At mys - ter - ies so bright.
Fair flowers of Par - a - dise ex - tend Their fra - grance ev - er sweet.
Your praise and glo - ry shall not fail Through-out e - ter - ni - ty.

Text: Rev. 19:12,; St. 1, 3-5, Matthew Bridges, 1800-1894; St. 2, Godfrey Thring, 1823-1903
Tune: DIADEMATA, SMD.; George J. Elvey, 1816-1893

For the Beauty of the Earth

1. For the beau-ty of the earth, For the glo-ry of the skies,
2. For the beau-ty of each hour Of the day and of the night,
3. For the joy of ear and eye, For the heart and mind's de-light,
4. For the joy of hu-man love, Broth-er, sis-ter, par-ent, child,

For the love which from our birth O-ver and a-round us lies:
Hill and vale, and tree and flow'r, Sun and moon, and stars of light:
For the mys-tic har-mon-y Link-ing sense to sound and sight:
Friends on earth, and friends a-bove; For all gen-tle thoughts and mild:

Refrain
Lord of all, to you we raise This our hymn of grate-ful praise.

Text: Folliet S. Pierpont, 1835-1917
Tune: DIX, 77 77 77; Arr. from Conrad Kocher, 1786-1872

63

God, Whose Almighty Word

1. God, whose al - might - y word Cha - os and dark - ness heard, And took their flight: Hear us, we hum - bly pray, And where the gos - pel - day Sheds not its glo - rious ray, Let there be light!

2. Sav - ior, you came to give Those who in dark - ness live Heal - ing and sight, Health to the sick in mind, Sight to the in - ward blind: Now to all hu - man - kind Let there be light!

3. Spir - it of truth and love, Life - giv - ing, ho - ly dove, Speed on your flight! Move on the wa - ter's face Bear - ing the lamp of grace And, in earth's dark - est place, Let there be light!

4. Gra - cious and ho - ly Three, Glo - ri - ous Trin - i - ty, Wis - dom, love, might: Bound - less as o - cean's tide Roll - ing in full - est pride Through the world far and wide, Let there be light!

Text: John Marriott, 1780-1825, alt.
Tune: ITALIAN HYMN, 66 4 666 4; Felice De Giardini, 1716-1796

Holy God, We Praise Thy Name

1. Ho - ly God, we praise thy name!
2. Hark! the loud ce - les - tial hymn
3. Ho - ly Fa - ther, Ho - ly Son,

Lord of all, we bow be - fore thee;
An - gel choirs a - bove are rais - ing;
Ho - ly Spir - it, Three we name thee,

All on earth thy scep - ter claim,
Cher - u - bim and Ser - a - phim
While in es - sence on - ly One,

All in heav'n a - bove a - dore thee;
In un - ceas - ing cho - rus prais - ing,
Un - di - vid - ed God we claim thee,

In - fi - nite thy vast do - main,
Fill the heav'ns with sweet ac - cord:
And a - dor - ing bend the knee,

Repeat ad lib

Ev - er - last - ing is thy reign.
Ho - ly, ho - ly, ho - ly Lord!
While we own the mys - ter - y.

Text: *Grosser Gott, wir loben dich*; Ascr. to Ignaz Franz, 1719-1790; Tr. by Clarence Walworth 1820-1900
Tune: GROSSER GOTT, 7 8 7 8 77: *Katholisches Gesangbuch*, Vienna, c. 1774

Holy, Holy, Holy! Lord God Almighty

1. Ho-ly, Ho-ly, Ho-ly! Lord God Al-might-y!
2. Ho-ly, Ho-ly, Ho-ly! all the saints a-dore thee,
3. Ho-ly, Ho-ly, Ho-ly! though the dark-ness hide thee,
4. Ho-ly, Ho-ly, Ho-ly! Lord God Al-might-y!

Ear-ly in the morn-ing our song shall rise to thee:
Cast-ing down their gold-en crowns a-round the glass-y sea;
Though the eye made blind by sin thy glo-ry may not see,
All thy works shall praise thy Name in earth, and sky, and sea;

Ho-ly, Ho-ly, Ho-ly! mer-ci-ful and might-y,
Cher-u-bim and ser-a-phim fall-ing down be-fore thee,
On-ly thou art ho-ly; there is none be-side thee,
Ho-ly, Ho-ly, Ho-ly! mer-ci-ful and might-y,

God in three Per-sons, bless-ed Trin-i-ty.
God ev-er-last-ing through e-ter-ni-ty.
Per-fect in power, in love, and pu-ri-ty.
God in three Per-sons, bless-ed Trin-i-ty.

Text: Reginald Heber, 1783-1826, alt.
Tune: NICAEA, 11 12 12 10; John B. Dykes, 1823-1876

66

I Heard the Voice of Jesus Say

1. I heard the voice of Je-sus say, "Come un-to me and rest;
2. I heard the voice of Je-sus say, "Be hold, I free-ly give
3. I heard the voice of Je-sus say, "I am this dark world's light;

Lay down, O wea-ry one, lay down Your head up-on my breast."
The liv-ing wa-ter; thirst-y one, Stoop down, and drink, and live."
Look un-to me, your morn shall rise, And all your day be bright."

I came to Je-sus as I was, So wea-ry worn and sad;
I came to Je-sus, and I drank Of that life-giv-ing stream;
I looked to Je-sus, and I found In him my star, my sun;

I found in him a rest-ing place, And he has made me glad.
My thirst was quenched, my soul re-vived, And now I live in him.
And in that light of life I'll walk Till trav-'ling days are done.

Text: Horatius Bonar, 1808-1889
Tune: KINGSFOLD, CMD; English

67

Immortal, Invisible, God Only Wise

		C		D		G	D	G
1.	Im -	mor - tal,	in -	vis - i - ble,	God	on - ly		wise,
2.	Un -	rest - ing,	un -	hast - ing, and	si -	lent	as	light,
3.	Life -	giv - ing	Cre -	a - tor, of	both	great and		small;
4.	Great	Fa - ther	of	glo - ry, pure	Fa -	ther	of	light,

	C		D		G	D	G
In	light	in - ac -	ces - si - ble	hid	from	our	eyes,
Nor	want - ing,	nor	wast - ing, you	rule	day	and	night;
Of	all	life the	mak - er, the	true	life	of	all;
Your	an - gels	a -	dor - ing, all	veil -	ing	their	sight;

	Bm		Em		Bm		D
Most	bless - ed,	most	glo - rious, the	An -	cient	of	Days,
Your	jus - tice	like	moun - tains high	soar -	ing	a -	bove
We	blos - som,	then	with - er as	leaves	on	a	tree,
We	too,	God in -	vis - i - ble,	of -	fer	our	praise;

	C		D		G	D	G
Al -	might - y,	vic -	to - rious, your	great	name	we	praise.
Your	clouds	which are	foun - tains of	good -	ness	and	love.
But	you	live for -	ev - er, who	is	and	will	be.
O	light	in - ac -	ces - si - ble,	An -	cient	of	Days!

Text: 1 Tim. 1:17; Walter C. Smith, 1824-1908, alt.
Tune: ST DENIO, 11 11 11 11; Roberts' *Canaidau y Cyssegr,* 1893

Love Divine, All Loves Excelling

1. Love di - vine, all loves ex - cel - ling, Joy of
2. Come, al - might - y to de - liv - er, Let us
3. Fin - ish then your new cre - a - tion, Pure and

heav'n to earth come down! Fix in us your
all your life re - ceive; Sud - den - ly re -
spot - less, gra - cious Lord. Let us see your

hum - ble dwell - ing, All your faith - ful mer - cies crown.
turn and nev - er, Nev - er more your tem - ples leave.
great sal - va - tion Per - fect - ly in you re - stored.

Je - sus, source of all com - pas - sion, Love un -
Lord, we would be al - ways bless - ing, Serve you
Changed from glo - ry in - to glo - ry, Till in

bound - ed love all pure; Vis - it us with
as your hosts a - bove, Pray, and praise you
heav'n we take our place, Till we sing be -

your sal - va - tion, Let your love in us en - dure.
with - out ceas - ing, Glo - ry in your pre - cious love.
fore the al - might - y Lost in won - der, love and praise.

Text: Charles Wesley, 1707-1788. alt.
Tune: HYFRYDOL, 8 7 8 7 D; Rowland H. Prichard, 1811-1887

Now Thank We All Our God

1. Now thank we all our God With hearts and hands and voic - es,
2. O may this gra - cious God Through all our life be near us,
3. All praise and thanks to God The Fa - ther now be giv - en,

Who won-drous things has done, In whom this world re - joic - es;
With ev - er joy - ful hearts And bless - ed peace to cheer us;
The Son, and Spir - it blest, Who reigns in high-est heav - en,

Who, from our moth-er's arms, Hath blessed us on our way
Pre - serve us in his grace, And guide us in dis - tress,
E - ter - nal, Tri - une God, Whom earth and heav'n a - dore;

With count-less gifts of love, And still is ours to - day.
And free us from all sin, Till heav-en we pos - sess.
For thus it was, is now, And shall be ev - er - more.

Text: *Nun danket alle Gott*; Martin Rinkart, 1586-1649; Tr. by Catherine Winkworth, 1827-1878, alt.
Tune: NUN DANKET, 6 7 6 7 6 6 6 6; Johann Crüger, 1598-1662

O God, Our Help in Ages Past

1. O God, our help in ages past,
   Our hope for years to come,
   Our shelter from the storm - y blast,
   And our e - ter - nal home.

2. Un - der the shad - ow of your throne
   Your saints have dwelt se - cure;
   Suf - fi - cient is your arm a - lone,
   And our de - fense is sure.

3. Be - fore the hills in or - der stood,
   Or earth re - ceived its frame,
   From ev - er - last - ing you are God,
   To end - less years the same.

4. A thou - sand a - ges in your sight
   Are like an eve - ning gone,
   Short as the watch that ends the night
   Be - fore the ris - ing sun.

5. Time, like an ever-rolling stream,
   Soon bears us all away;
   We fly forgotten, as a dream
   Dies at the op'ning day.

6. O God, our help in ages past,
   Our hope for years to come,
   Still be our guard while troubles last,
   And our eternal home.

Text: Psalm (89)90; Isaac Watts, 1674-1748
Tune: ST. ANNE, CM; Attr. to William Croft, 1678-1727

Praise to the Lord, the Almighty

1. Praise to the Lord, the Al - might-y, the king of cre - a - tion!
2. Praise to the Lord, a - bove all things so might - i - ly reign - ing,
3. Praise to the Lord, who shall pros - per our work and de - fend us;
4. Praise to the Lord - O let all that is in us a - dore him!

O my soul, praise him, for he is your health and sal - va - tion!
Keep-ing us safe at his side, and so gent - ly sus - tain - ing.
Sure - ly his good-ness and mer - cy shall dai - ly at - tend us.
All that has life and breath come now with prais - es be - fore him!

Come, all who hear: Broth - ers and sis - ters, draw near,
Have you not seen All you have need - ed has been
Pon - der a - new What the Al - might - y can do,
Let the "A - men!" Sound from his peo - ple a - gain —

Praise him in glad ad - o - ra - tion!
Met by his gra - cious or - dain - ing?
Who with his love will be - friend us.
Glad - ly with praise we a - dore him!

Text: *Lobe den Herren, den mächtigen König*; Joachim Meander, 1650-1680; Tr. by Catherine Winkworth, 1827-1878, alt.
Tune: LOBE DEN HERREN, 14 14 47 8; Straslund Gesangbuch, 1665

There's a Wideness in God's Mercy

1. There's a wide-ness in God's mer-cy Like the wide-ness of the sea;
2. For the love of God is broad-er Than the meas-ures of our mind,
3. Trou-bled souls, why will you scat-ter Like a crowd of fright-ened sheep?

There's a kind-ness in God's jus-tice Which is more than lib-er-ty.
And the heart of the E-ter-nal Is most won-der-ful-ly kind.
Fool-ish hearts, why will you wan-der From a love so true and deep?

There is plen-ti-ful re-demp-tion In the blood that has been shed;
If our love were but more sim-ple We should take him at his word,
There is wel-come for the sin-ner And more grac-es for the good;

There is joy for all the mem-bers In the sor-rows of the Head.
And our lives would be thanks-giv-ing For the good-ness of our Lord.
There is mer-cy with the Sav-ior, There is heal-ing in his blood.

Text: Frederick W. Faber, 1814-1863, alt.
Tune: IN BABILONE, 8 7 8 7 D; *Oude en Nieuwe Hollanste Boerenlities*, c. 1710

When I Survey the Wondrous Cross

1. When I sur - vey the won - drous cross
2. For - bid it, Lord, that I should boast
3. See, from his head, his hands, his feet,
4. Were the whole realm of na - ture mine,

On which the prince of glo - ry died,
Save in the death of Christ, my God;
Sor - row and love flow min - gled down;
That were a pre - sent far too small:

My rich - est gain I count but loss
All the vain things that charm me most,
Did e'er such love and sor - row meet,
Love so a - maz - ing so di - vine,

And pour con - tempt on all my pride.
I sac - ri - fice them to his blood.
Or thorns com - pose so rich a crown?
De - mands my soul, my life, my all.

Text: Isaac Watts, 1676-1748
Tune: HAMBURG , Lowell Mason, 1792-1872